AF445697

مُغامَرَة في المنْطاد

تأليف: ميساء موسى

رسوم: نور التوبة

دار الرُّقيّ
للطباعة والنشر والتوزيع

إهـــداء

إلى كلِّ أطْفالِ العالَم،
إلى كلِّ مَنْ كانَ سَنَدًا لي
ويَدْعَمُني مِنْ عائِلَتي وأصدِقائي

طَلَبَتِ الآنِسَة «عُلا» مِنْ تَلامِيذِها أَنْ يَتَحَدَّثَ كُلٌّ مِنْهُم عَنْ مُغامَرَةٍ يُفَضِّلُها.

«سُهى» تُحِبُّ أَنْ تَرْكَبَ الطّائِرَة، «مَجْد» يُحِبُّ أَنْ يَرْكَبَ السَّفِينَة،

«سَلمى» تُحِبُّ أَنْ تَتَزَلَّجَ عَلى الجَلِيد، لَكِنَّ مُغامَرَةَ «سامِر» كانَتْ مُمَيَّزَةٌ فَهُوَ يُحِبُّ أَنْ يَرْكَبَ المِنْطاد.

7

«جَميلٌ جِدًّا يا أوْلاد!»، هَكَذا قالَتِ الآنِسَة «عُلا».

فَـ «سُهى» تَسْتَمْتِعُ كَثيرًا بِمُشاهَدَةِ أفْلامٍ عَنِ الطّائِرَة، وتَأْتي إلى الصَّفِّ وتُخبِرُ رِفاقَها كَيْفَ أخَذَها والِدُها إلى المَطارِ وشاهَدَتِ الطّائِرَةُ كَيْفَ تَطيرُ في السَّماء.

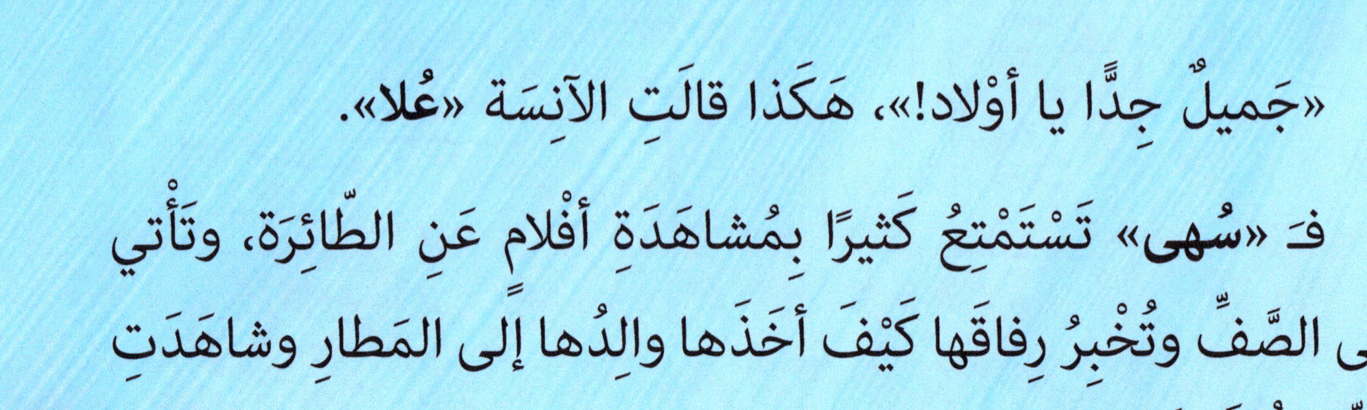

«مَجْد» يَرْكَبُ السَّفينَةَ مَعَ والِدِهِ فَهُوَ بَحَّارٌ وَيَسْتَمْتِعُ كَثيرًا بِرُؤْيَةِ البَحْرِ مِنْ حَوْلِه. «سَلمى» تُحِبُّ التَّزَلُّجَ عَلى الجَليدِ وَلَدَيْها زَلّاجَاتٍ لَكِنّها ما زالَتْ تَتَدَرَّبُ عَلَيْها لِتُشارِكَ في «مُسابَقَةِ الجَليد».

أمّا «سامِر» فَمُغامَرَتُهُ لَيْسَتْ كَباقي المُغامَراتِ فَهُوَ يُحِبُّ رُكوبَ المِنْطاد، لَكِنَّ والِدَهُ يَرْفُضُ أَنْ يَأْخُذَهُ بِرِحْلَةٍ في هَذا المِنْطادِ العَجيب.

فَكُلُّ صَديقٍ لَهُ يَسْتَمْتِعُ بِالمُغامَرَةِ الَّتي يُحِبّ.

وكانَتِ الآنِسَة «عُلا» تُلاحِظُ حُبَّهُ لِلمِنْطاد، فَهُوَ يَتَمَنَّى الرَّكوبَ بِهِ حَتَّى يَرى البَحْر، البُيوت، والأَشْجارَ مِنْ أَعْلى، يُحِبُّ أَنْ يَرى شَكْلَها مِنْ بَعيدٍ.

The Cycle

3 years
Since the healing process began
3 years
Since we talked
2.5 years
Since I started seeking help
2 years
Since I got the job of my dreams
1 year
Since I fell into another trap
6 months
Since everything fell apart
1 month
Since the healing process began

gender
A vast
Fluid
Moving
Sea
Of expression
Experience
Effervescent
Unequivocally my own

My body
Is not a crime scene
My expression
Is not an offense
My presentation
Is not a danger
My medication
Is not optional
My operations
Are not mutilation
My body
Will not be regulated
My presence
Will not be erased

Them
Is plural
Because I'm not a singular
a multitude
also nothing
on the outside
And In the fringes
In the in betweens
And the spaces beyond
In your hopes
In dreams
Our future
And past

I fell for you
In college
In class
Later at the library
Again at coffee
Then again when you wrote me notes
That time we shared a fitting room
When we got tipsy
And giggled and took pictures like it was date
In your letters you said you loved me
I wrote back how beautiful you were
But we both "knew" that "it" was "wrong"
we also didn't know what "it" was
Or could've been
You married him
I stood by you
Watched you vow away your life
And it all faded
You faded
As I fell
From grace
Out of your life
A dusty photo in a drawer
a memory
A mess of words on a page

From my queer heart to yours

Inflation caught up with me
before my dreams could even be realized
young me thought a degree would be plenty
now I see the lies

Give god another try
Absolutely...Not

Unraveling
Once tattered
Now torn
Once looped
trimmed
bordered
Neatly hemmed
Now mangled
Tangled
Undone
Limp
Strings dangle
Unspun
Each little agitation
And movement
Makes way
Once delicate yarn
Now frayed
Leaving me
My whole self
Full display

Some places
Send chills
Invoke nausea
Heaviness
Haunted by a million ghosts
Ghouls
Demons
Past me
What was
What could have been
What will never be
Memories
Should haves
What ifs
Wounds

Alan
I'm not Barbie
Not Ken
I'm not pink
Not sparkly
Not new
Or well known
They have tried to discontinue me
But I live on

It's not yours
It's not fair
To bear the brunt
Or carry the burden
Of how others perceive you.
But nonetheless
You strain
Under the weight
Societal norms
Stares
Whispers
Outrage
Violence
It's not your job
To manage feelings that don't belong to you
But you tread carefully
You're allowed to exist
Or live your truth
Ideally both
If you resist
Ideally both

Love, polyamory, and ADHD
I worry constantly
That I'm forgetting
Or too distracted
Rolling in
Bouncing out
A hundred calendars
Trying not to leave you out
I see the new and shiny
Hyperfixations
Odd priorities
Long quiet stretches
And I know how it looks
I promised each of you
To try not to let you down
Too much

Head down
Shoulders back
Knees on the floor
And at the toe of my boot
Eyes on me now
Ears follow my commands
Mouth gagged
Nose to leather
Good, pet

The best
My best
Your best
Don't exist
But we continue to try

T4T

A swipe right
Two otters in a world of possibilities
A masc that matches mine
kindred souls and bodies
Connected by fate
Intertwined with joy
refreshment to my parched lips

A name
My great grandmother
And a pop hit
My parents' inspiration
I still carry the gift on paper
And in frames
But that person is not me
"She" is Outdated
Outgrown
And buried

Fluorescent lights
Buzzing
Chatter
Clacking keys
Busy
Email
Post it notes
Earphones block
overstimulation
Commute
Traffic
Stay on time
You're needed at your desk
Deadlines
Tickets
All hands meeting
Catered lunch
"Be grateful"
"At least you have a job"

T4T pt 2
euphoric sounds
As bodies meet
hands explore
in security and solace
beyond binary
beyond roles
beyond expectations
Pleasure and joy
Belong to us, too

Pronouns
Pins
Signature
Introductions
It's exhausting
Everytime you "forget"
Or worse ignore it
thorns poke through my soul
Stop apologizing
Start doing better

Rae learned to read at age four and has been immersed in books ever since. They have a Bachelor of Arts in English and this is their full collection of poetry so far. They hope there is more to come.